Table Of Contents

Introduction

Did you ever wonder why a person sitting next to you in the office chooses to work as an independent computer consultant while telling you that he/she is not getting any benefits such health insurance, paid vacation and sick leave? The answer is very simple and may surprise you. This person is doing it because he/she is making 50-100% more than you are while doing the same exact work.

At the same time this person does not have to worry about office politics, size of the annual bonus and whether or not he/she will be getting a promotion. The reason for this is rather simple; all this person really cares and worries about is this person's hourly rate that he/she is getting for every hour that he/she is working.

In addition to making 50-100% more than a permanent employee independent consultant, depending on contractual status, gets to deduct various items as business expenses such as cell phone, home internet connection, tolls for traveling between client sites as well as gets to make bigger tax deductible contributions to 401k style plans.[1]

Also, whenever independent consultant does not like the project he/she is working on they can, assuming

---

[1] Each person's tax situation is different. Please consult your CPA for tax advice specific to your situation.

contractual obligations have been met, switch to another project without worrying that a 6 months "job" will look bad on their resume.

Recently due to economic conditions many large companies decided on "hiring" independent consultants instead of permanent employees since independent consultants are not included in the company's official headcount that is reported to the Wall Street during quarterly earnings calls.

Working as an independent computer consultant can be very lucrative financially as well as personally since this work arrangement allows for greater variety of projects and locations.

TIP #1: Understand why companies hire Independent Consultants

There are several reasons why companies hire independent computer consultants some of which are purely political and therefore even more important to be aware of:

1. The company does not have expertise in a certain IT area
2. The company does not have enough staff to complete the project on time
3. Hiring manager does not want to go through HR department to hire employee and deal with a month long approval and hiring process
4. Due to hiring freeze the company cannot hire permanent employees, however it still needs someone to get the work done and independent consultants are not included in the company's headcount
5. The salary that company has to pay in order to get an expert in a certain field is higher than manager's salary. Therefore the company will hire an independent consultant so they would not have to break the corporate pay scale structure.

TIP #2: How to write Independent computer consultant resume

The overall structure of a "regular" resume used to find permanent employment and an "independent computer consultant" resume is the same. However, there are several differences that are important to understand.

The rule for a regular resume is to try to keep it to one page and not to exceed 2 pages. Such format will not work for independent consultant resume and in many cases a 2 page resume for a consultant might look "bad" and give an impression of inexperience to the manager reviewing it. I am not suggesting that you should have a 10 page resume hoping that its weight will get you an interview but a 5 – 6 page resume is quite common for independent computer consultants.

On the first page of the resume you will need to summarize your experience in 3 – 5 lines:

Senior consultant with extensive experience in designing and developing large scale accounting systems for a Fortune 100 manufacturing company, a major communications company and a regional bank utilizing latest client server and Web technologies.

Next list all special technical skills, software packages, programming languages etc. that you are an expert in.

Then you can list all jobs/projects that you have worked on.

Keep in mind that as an independent computer consultant you do not need to worry about short term assignments/jobs that you have had. Try to emphasize areas of your experience in which you would prefer your next project to be in.

TIP #3: Understand differences between working on W2, 1099 and Corp to Corp (C2C)[1]

Whenever you look at a job posting for an independent computer consultant position you will notice that it always mentions one of the following 3 terms W2, 1099 and Corp to Corp (C2C).

It is extremely important to understand what they actually mean and advantages and disadvantages of each one.

W2

When you work on a W2 you are basically a temporary employee of the consulting company/agency. The arrangement is similar to working as a regular permanent employee on a W2 in the sense that the agency takes out taxes out of your payroll check, however the major difference is that in most cases you are not eligible in participating on agency's benefits programs such as health insurance, 401k etc.

The major advantage of working on W2 is that in most states once your contract is over and since, in the eyes of the government, you have been an employee of the

---

[1] Each person's tax situation is different. Please consult your CPA for tax advice specific to your situation.

agency you can apply for unemployment benefits while you are looking for your next contract[1].

However, there are 2 major disadvantages to working on a W2 contract:

1. Since your agency has to pay employer's portion of FICA taxes as well as Workers Compensation and Unemployment taxes the hourly rate that agency pays to you will be substantially lower sometimes as much as $10-$15/hour.
2. Depending on your situation deducting work related expenses such as cellular phone, home internet service etc. maybe difficult, if not impossible.
3. Unless your agency offers 401k plan to temporary employees/independent consultants your ability to participate in tax advantaged retirement plan is very limited.

1099

1099 is a tax form that agency will mail to you and IRS to show how much money they paid to you during the year. The form is similar to 1099 you get from your bank showing how much interest income bank paid to you during the year. Agency does not deduct any taxes from your earnings and it is therefore your responsibility to pay all taxes that you owe to the government.

---

[1] Please consult your state's Labor Department for your state's laws and regulations.

Advantages of working on 1099:
1. Since the agency through which you work does not have to pay payroll taxes you can usually negotiate a much higher, sometimes $10-$15/hour, rate.
2. When you work on a 1099 you are considered to be self employed which means you are in a business for yourself. Since you are now a business, business related expenses such as home office, cellular phone, internet connection, laptop etc are tax deductible.
3. You can open your own 401k style plan and contribute significant amounts of money to it.

Disadvantages of working on 1099:
1. Since you are self employed, in most states, you are no longer eligible to apply for unemployment benefits once your contract ends.
2. In addition to income tax you now have to pay the FICA (Social Security and Medicare) tax on your entire income after business expenses which is 15.3%. More details about this tax can be found on IRS website http://ssa-custhelp.ssa.gov/cgi-bin/ssa.cfg/php/enduser/std_adp.php?p_faqid=172

Corp to Corp (C2C)
Corp to Corp refers to situations when one corporation (agency) is paying another corporation (corporation that

you own) for your services as an independent consultant. This is different from W2 and 1099 contracts which are between a corporation (agency) and individual (independent computer consultant).

In order to utilize this arrangement you will need to open and legally register you own corporation. You can do this yourself or your accountant can do it for you, fees are usually under $500.

For further discussion the assumption is that you decided or your accountant recommended that you open S Corporation. S Corporation laws and regulations are beyond the scope of this book. Please read the following for more information
http://en.wikipedia.org/wiki/S_corporation

Advantages of working on C2C:
1. Since the agency through which you work does not have to pay payroll taxes you can usually negotiate a much higher, sometimes $10-$15/hour, rate.
2. When you own a corporation it can incur business expenses just like any other business. Therefore, business related expenses such as cellular phone, internet connection, laptop etc are tax deductible on the corporate tax return.
3. Corporation can open its own 401k style plan and contribute significant amounts of money to it.
4. The major advantage of S Corporation over 1099 is that FICA (Social Security and Medicare) tax is

payable only on portion of your income that corporation pays to you as a salary. The rest of the income can be paid to you as corporate dividends which are not subject to 15.3% FICA tax.

Disadvantages of working on C2C:

1. Since you will be an officer of a corporation, in most states, you are no longer eligible to apply for unemployment benefits once your contract ends.

Because of the advantages mentioned above most independent computer consultant prefer to work on a Corp to Corp contracts.

TIP #4: Understand relationship between client, recruiter and consultant

Understanding relationship between a client, recruiter and a consultant is one of the key things you need to understand in order to be successful independent consultant.

There are three reasons why large companies use recruiters instead of hiring consultants directly:

1. When the time comes to pay consultants at the end of the month it is easier for a company to deal with 2-3 agencies and pay 2-3 invoices instead of dealing with tens if not hundreds of consultants and invoices.
2. Since the payment goes through the agency the company does not have to worry about having independent consultant being reclassified from independent contractor to employee by IRS and having to pay tens of thousands of dollars in payroll taxes and penalties. For more read IRS Publication 1779 http://www.irs.gov/pub/irs-pdf/p1779.pdf
3. Since recruiting is their primary business supposedly agencies can find better and cheaper consultants.

Agencies make money by billing the client a higher hourly rate than they pay the consultant. The usual commission for a "corp to corp" (C2C) and 1099 arrangements is 20-25%. For W2 arrangements the split is usually 30-35%. As you can see there is a lot of money involved and agencies commission depends on their ability to charge the company as much as possible while paying the consultant as little as possible. It is not uncommon for the agency to bill the client $100/hour and then pay the consultant $50/hour on a C2C "due to weak market demand" for consultant's skills.

This is exactly the opposite of the usual employment agency arrangement where the agency gets 20-25% of new employee's annual salary and is therefore interested in getting the candidate as high a salary as possible.

At the same time agency would rather have consultant working and bringing in small commission rather than not make money at all and see the position get filled by a competitor.

Therefore, one of the biggest secrets that staffing agencies have is the billing rate that they charge the client for consultant's services. With time most consultants find out what the billing rate is either by talking to client's manager or seeing agency's invoice on a fax machine.

Understanding the above relationship and knowing how recruiters function and make money is one of the most important things in being an independent computer consultant.

Bonus Tip: Once you find out that the billing rate is outrageously high don't be afraid to ask your agency for a raise. They will give it to you without much hassle because they would rather make $10/hour than nothing.

TIP #5: How to save time and find projects faster

One of the least used features of job search websites are search agents. They are a great tool which will do most of the job search for you.

Once you set up a user account on job search website such as Dice, Monster, HotJobs or any other there is an option to create a search agent or email alert. You provide the criteria for the alert such as keyword or skill, desired location, rate expectation, contract or permanent etc. same way as if you were searching manually. You then save the alert and it will email to you new job postings that match search criteria that you specified. You can set up multiple alerts under different names such as Java contracts Boston or COBOL contracts New Jersey.

It is best to set up the alerts to run on daily basis so you will get updates every day. Some websites run alerts at night when there is least amount of users, however some sites will run alert at the time when it was created. Therefore, it is best to create alerts either late at night or early in the morning. This way you can check your email once in the morning and apply to all new jobs that were posted during previous day.

Another very useful feature of the search agents is the ability to specify that you only want NEW job postings emailed to you. This will save you a lot of time since many recruiters like to update their postings with non important details so that they will appear at the top of search results as if they were new.

Also, there are websites such as www.indeed.com that aggregate search results from multiple job search websites, newspapers, magazines and forums and combine them in one website. Indeed also has the ability to set up email search agent however since it will be picking up results from multiple sites search criteria is limited.

Another nice feature of Indeed is their trends report which provides very good picture of demand for certain job skills.

These reports can be accessed through the following links:

Overall job market
http://www.indeed.com/jobtrends/industry

IT job market
http://www.indeed.com/jobtrends/information-technology-industry

Search for specific skill in a specific location
http://www.indeed.com/jobtrends?q=Java+Chicago&l=

TIP #6: Let the recruiters find you instead of you looking for them

Another rarely or even not correctly used feature of job search websites is the opportunity to post your resume online.

Most people either do not upload their resume to websites fearing that their boss, co-worker or competitor will see it or post a full 10 page version with all personal identifying information.

What I found works best is posting limited personal identification information and a summary of your resume.

For example:
- Instead of posting your full name you can use an abbreviation of your last name
- Instead of including your company name you can say "major financial services firm" or "Fortune 500 manufacturing company"
- Instead of posting several pages, which recruiters will not read anyway, post a summary of your major skills and accomplishments

Also, since most recruiters do a keyword search and most do not know the difference between C++ and C# include as many "industry buzzwords" as possible in your summary.

Bonus tip:
Make sure your email address sounds professional. Trying to become independent consultant and having your email as sunflower@yahoo.com is not a good idea. Also, make sure your voicemail message is professional as well and doesn't have screaming kids in the background.

TIP #7: Screen recruiters before you decide to work with them

This tip might sound strange and illogical at first. Why would you turn down someone who is calling you and offering you a possible job/project?

There is a very simple reason you want to do that. Most companies especially large ones have what is called a Vendors List. It is a list of approved vendors that the company contacts whenever it needs to find an independent computer consultant. Usually companies on the vendor list are relatively large national agencies. They are sometimes called Tier 1 vendors and the open position is referred to "job req."

Depending on the complexity of client's requirements, job market and how busy agency is filling other jobs Tier 1 agency might decide to subcontract job req to a Tier 2 agency which is usually a regional firm or a specialized firm. Tier 2 agency for its own reasons might give this job req to a Tier 3 agency which could be someone working out of their basement or a firm that has an office in US but whose recruiting department is outsourced to another country.

At this point it is quite obvious that Tier 2 and Tier 3 agencies need to make money somehow. The only way they can do that is by paying the consultant a lower rate for the work that he/she will be doing. It is not unusual for

Tier 2 and Tier 3 agencies to take a $10/hour cut EACH. Assuming that consultant works a whole year on a project that translates into $40,000 that consultant will not get for his/her work.

It is not unusual for the same job req to be advertised by 10 different agencies on websites such as Dice. Therefore it is very important when you get a call from a recruiter to find out where in the Tier structure they are. Most will not tell the truth and claim that they are direct (Tier 1) with client. The easiest way I found to screen out Tier 2 and Tier 3 agencies right away is to ask them what kind of a rate they are paying. Usually the rate is unreasonably low and you can tell the caller right away that you are not interested in the project.

TIP #8: Do not get "double-submitted"

Because of the Tier structure described above it is very easy to get submitted for the same position by 2-3 different agencies at the same time. Counter to thinking that this will improve your chances of getting the project this will actually eliminate you from the applicant pool.

You will be eliminated because if the client company hires you it will have to determine which of the 2-3 agencies that submitted you should get a commission. This can potentially open the client company to lawsuits from agencies that did not get their commission. Since the hiring manager doesn't want to deal with such exposure he/she will eliminate you from the candidate pool.

Therefore is you have been submitted to a company by one agency and another one wants to submit you as well you should tell them right away that you have already been submitted.

TIP #9: Skip agency interview

Some agents when they first talk to you will tell you that they need to interview you before they can submit your resume to the client. It is true that some clients have an agency interview as a screening requirement, however what I found is that agency interviews are usually useless and are a big waste of time.

Over the last 10 years not a single agency where I had an interview was able to find me a project. On the other hand, I have never met some of the agents that found projects for me since all communication, including signing the contract, was done over the phone, fax and email.

Majority of agents that ask you to come in for an interview are junior people who were told that this is a process by their managers. Senior recruiters know that agency interview is a waste of time for both themselves as well as the candidate and therefore prefer to ask questions that they have over the phone.

Therefore, next time recruiter asks you to come in for a "face to face" interview ask him/her if it can be done over the phone. If the recruiter still insists you can say that you are very busy with your current project and will not be able to take time off until next week. Since recruiters work on commission they will do everything they can to get your resume to the client without meeting you in person first.

TIP #10: What to do about short term contracts?

When you first speak to a recruiter about a project one of the key questions to ask is what is the duration of a project.

There are 3 general types of project duration:
1. 2-3 weeks project
2. 3 months project
3. 6+ months project

The 2 - 3 week project is usually "sky is about to fall project." This means that the project is behind a deadline or current staff cannot complete portion of the project due to lack of knowledge. It is up to each individual to decide whether they want to deal with such a project but if you do decide to take it you can ask for a higher rate than usual.

3 months contracts are not as bad as they sound. I have seen 3 months contracts turn into 2 – 3 year contracts. Basically, most 3 months contracts are really trial periods for a consultant. Since the screening process to hire independent computer consultant is usually not as rigorous as for permanent employees, hiring manager is just protecting himself/herself. If consultant does not perform, manager does not have to renew the contract and thus avoid "firing" consultant and associated hard feelings. On the other if everything works out well most

contracts have a clause that "at the end of original contract duration it is renewable under the same terms unless terminated in writing."

6+ months projects are similar to 3 months ones except that the hiring manager is comfortable bringing in a consultant for longer duration.